A LITTLE GUIDE TO

Birds

DANIELLE BELLENY

T0364080

RP Minis®
Hachette Book Group
1290 Avenue of the Americas, New York, NY 10104
www.runningpress.com
@Running_Press

First Edition: April 2022

Published by RP Minis, an imprint of Perseus Books, LLC, a
subsidiary of Hachette Book Group, Inc. The RP Minis name
and logo is a registered trademark of the Hachette Book Group.

The Hachette Speakers Bureau provides a wide range of
authors for speaking events. To find out more, go to
www.hachettespeakersbureau.com or call (866) 376-6591.

The publisher is not responsible for websites (or their
content) that are not owned by the publisher.

ISBN: 978-0-7624-7598-8

HOW THE WORLD
GOT BIRDS

Let's start with some great news. If you thought you were 65 million years too late to experience dinosaurs, think again. Dinosaurs still walk among us. So where are they? Surprisingly, many—possibly even most—people encounter them daily, and not as lizards, as you might think. Instead, these modern-day dinosaurs come to you and me as birds. In this mini book, you'll learn a bit about how to find birds to watch, as well as the common names, scientific names, and habitats of the birds featured in your new set of wooden bird magnets and on this book cover.

HOW TO FIND BIRDS

Luckily for us, birds are found almost everywhere on the planet. They live on all seven continents, and there are even bird species that spend a significant portion of their lives flying over oceans, thousands of miles offshore. Finding a bird can be as simple as observing the birds right outside your window. But that's not to say birds are always easy to find.

Birding is like trying to collect all the special prizes from a cereal box. You never know what you'll find on a day of bird- ing, and you're not guaranteed the bird you most covet, but you'll prob- ably encounter some other really awesome species along the way. Birding can happen anywhere and at any time. Sure, parks exist, but have you watched birds in a parking lot?

A lake has plenty of sights to offer, but have you watched birds in a retention pond behind a shopping center? What is a cemetery but a park with extra architecture? Nature enthusiasts need not look further than their own home to enjoy the outdoors. Virtual birding is even an option. Livestreams can provide instant nature watching from bird feeders, nests, and watering holes across the world at any time of day. And since nature is always action-packed and full of drama, nature cams are great shows to have on in the background while you do other things. They can definitely help pass the time on a slow day at work.

While there are no bad birds, some birds do get labeled "trash birds." Haters will call them rats with wings. Birds that can be seen very readily and abundantly get the title of trash bird. The term *trash bird* can sometimes also be taken literally, with some such birds found unapologetically romping in the garbage. Trash birds shouldn't be deemed low in value, though, especially since the age-old adage "one person's trash is another person's treasure" holds true even in avian examples. Depending on your region, what you call a trash bird could be someone else's dream bird. Don't be discouraged from a deep appreciation for these species. Defend your regional trash bird mascot!

Birders are very adept at birding anywhere. When a birder tells you they "know a spot," be prepared to be taken to the back of an abandoned strip mall, a culvert on the side of the road, or the parking lot of an apartment complex to look for birds.

Birds have successfully integrated into human-altered landscapes, and watching them in an urban context is just as exciting as watching them in rural areas. If you're really game, it may be worth a trip to the trash dump. An excursion to the local landfill will often reward those brave adventurers with rare bird encounters. The mounds of trash in a landfill would deter most reasonable people, but they are buffet tables for birds. Food scraps, insects, and rodents can attract a range of species. If birding at a dump isn't your style, other popular yet offbeat birding hot spots include cemeteries. (You can go one step further and protect birds by getting a conservation burial, an all-natural style of burial that also helps conserve land. Prairie Creek Conservation in Florida is a great example of a conservation cemetery. As an added bonus, Prairie Creek Conservation offers 2,000 acres of protected land to explore in this life and the afterlife.)

Depending on your level of participation, birding can involve long-distance trips to see a rare species. Rare bird alerts notify birders of uncommon species that have recently been reported in an area. Depending on the rarity, enthusiasts from every corner of the world may travel to the spot just for a chance to see or hear their target species. Eco-tourism is one of the fastest-growing areas of the tourism economy, but it's not absolutely necessary to travel far and wide to see a bird. You can attract birds to your local patch with food and water. Better yet, fill the spaces near you with native flowers and shrubs. Birds can use the resources native plants provide year-round. The next rare bird that visits might be enticed to choose your yard as its new favorite spot.

Bird feeders come in a variety of styles that can meet your needs.

Birdseed comes in a variety of mixes that target certain birds. Save yourself the stress by skipping the mixes with fillers and give the birds what they really want: sunflower seeds, peanuts, and suet. Suet is a mix of solidified fat gathered from beef kidneys. It can be combined with birdseed, cut into thick slices called suet cakes, and attached by string to a tree branch for a lucky bird—or even luckier squirrel—to snack on. However, the texture is far from that of a cake; instead it is a dense brick of greasy fat with the consistency of a peanut butter cup. This familiar confectionery consistency makes suet cakes the forbidden candy bar. Despite the ingredients list, a bold thought to take a small bite from the suet cake will forever linger in the minds of devoted birders.

Be sure to regularly sanitize your bird feeders, birdbaths, and suet cake holders to avoid spreading salmonella, finch eye disease, and other diseases to animals. Centralized feeding locations are potential disease vectors if not maintained properly.

On the next pages, you will see examples of birds you might encounter in North America, including those on your new wooden magnets!

SELECTED BIRDS *of* NORTH AMERICA

BLUETHROAT

Scientific Name: Luscinia svecica

Habitat: Found in Alaska

GAMBEL'S QUAIL, AKA SONORAN QUAIL

Scientific Name: *Callipepla gambelii*

Habitat: Found in the southwestern United States and northern Mexico

GREEN JAY

Scientific Name: Cyanocorax yncas

Habitat: Found in southern Texas and eastern Mexico

HOODED WARBLER

Scientific Name: Setophaga citrina

Habitat: Found throughout North America

LUCIFER HUMMINGBIRD, AKA LUCIFER SHEARTAIL

Scientific Name: Calothorax lucifer

Habitat: Found in West Texas, Southern Arizona, southern New Mexico, and throughout central Mexico

NORTHERN CARDINAL

Scientific Name: Cardinalis cardinalis

Habitat: Found throughout eastern North America

NORTHERN JACANA

Scientific Name: Jacana spinosa

Habitat: Found along the Gulf and Pacific coasts of Mexico

PAINTED BUNTING

Scientific Name: Passerina ciris

Habitat: Found in the southern United States and throughout Mexico

ROCK PTARMIGAN

Scientific Name: *Lagopus muta*

Habitat: Found on the coasts of Greenland and throughout northern Canada and Alaska

ROSEATE SPOONBILL

Scientific Name: Platalea ajaja

Habitat: Found along the Gulf Coast shoreline of North America and the Pacific coast of Mexico

SNOWY OWL

Scientific Name: Bubo scandiacus

Habitat: Found throughout Canada, Alaska, and the northern United States

ZONE-TAILED HAWK

Scientific Name: Buteo albonotatus

Habitat: Found in the southern United States and throughout Mexico

This book has been bound using handcraft methods and Smyth-sewn to ensure durability.

The dust jacket and interior were illustrated by Stephanie Singleton and designed by Jenna McBride.

The text was written by Danielle Belleny.